SCIENCE ANSWERS

Green Plants

FROM ROOTS TO LEAVES

Louise and Richard Spilsbury

www.heinemann.co.uk/library
Visit our website to find out more information about **Heinemann Library** books.

To order:
☎ Phone 44 (0) 1865 888066
▤ Send a fax to 44 (0) 1865 314091
▢ Visit the Heinemann Bookshop at www.heinemann.co.uk/library to browse our catalogue and order online.

First published in Great Britain by Heinemann Library, Halley Court, Jordan Hill, Oxford OX2 8EJ, part of Harcourt Education.

Heinemann is a registered trademark of Harcourt Education Ltd.

Editorial: Nancy Dickmann and Tanvi Rai
Design: Richard Parker and Celia Floyd
Picture Research: Rebecca Sodergren and Pete Morris
Production: Séverine Ribierre

Originated by Dot Gradations Ltd
Printed in China by WKT Company Limited

ISBN 0 431 17512 8
08 07 06 05 04
10 9 8 7 6 5 4 3 2 1

British Library Cataloguing in Publication Data
Spilsbury, Louise and Richard
Green Plants. – (Science Answers)
580
A full catalogue record for this book is available from the British Library.

Acknowledgements
The publishers would like to thank the following for permission to reproduce photographs: Corbis/Chris Hellier **p. 12**; FLPA/Alwyn J. Roberts **p. 20**; FLPA/Colin Marshall **p. 25**; FLPA/Dr David Hosking **p. 5**; FLPA/Jurgen & Christine Sohns **p. 23**; FLPA/M Hollings **p. 21**; FLPA/Minden Pictures **p. 24**; Harcourt Education Ltd/Tudor Photography **pp. 10, 14, 22**; Holt Studios International **p. 8**; Nature Picture Library **p. 19**; NHPA/Ernie Janes **p. 15**; NHPA/G. I. Bernard **p. 7**; NHPA/Jane Gifford **p. 27**; NHPA/Jany Sauvanet **p. 16**; NHPA/Stephen Dalton **p. 17**; Science Photo Library **pp. 18, 28**; Science Photo Library/Adam Hart-Davis **p. 9**; Science Photo Library/Claude Nuridsany & Marie Perennou **p. 13**; Science Photo Library/David Nunuk **p. 29**; Science Photo Library/Dr Jeremy Burgess **p. 11**; Science Photo Library/Dr Morley Read **p. 4**; Science Photo Library/Simon Fraser **p. 26**.

Cover photograph of a tropical rainforest in Costa Rica reproduced with permission of NHPA/John Shaw.

Contents

Any words appearing in bold, **like this**, are explained in the Glossary.

About the experiments and demonstrations

This book contains some boxes headed 'Science Answers'. Each one describes an experiment or demonstration that you can try yourself. There are some simple safety rules to follow when doing an experiment:

- Ask an adult to help with any cutting using a sharp knife.
- Never play around with plastic bags.
- Wash your hands after touching plants and/or soil.

Materials you will use

Most of the experiments and demonstrations in this book can be done with objects that you can find in your own home and plants you can buy cheaply from a garden centre. You will also need a pencil and paper to record your results.

What are plants?

All the living things in the world can be divided into five large groups called **kingdoms**. Plants are one of the kingdoms of living things. There is a huge variety of plants in the world. Green plants are grouped together because they all trap **energy** from sunlight and use it to make food within their own bodies.

Why are plants green?

The **stems** and **leaves** of plants look green because they contain a green substance called **chlorophyll**. Chlorophyll captures light energy for plants to make their own food. Mushrooms and other **fungi** are not green plants because they do not contain chlorophyll and therefore they cannot make their own food.

The leaves of some green plants are different colours, such as red or yellow. Their leaves still contain chlorophyll, but another pigment (colour) in the leaves is stronger.

Towering trees

Trees are the mightiest plants. In the Amazonian rainforest like this one in Ecuador, South America, there may be over 750 species (kinds) of trees in a single square kilometre!

4

Producers and consumers

Plants are called **producers** because they produce their own food. Animals cannot do this – they are **consumers**. They eat plants, or other animals that eat plants, to get the energy they need to live and grow. This means that when an animal like a lion consumes a plant-eating animal like a zebra, the lion is still relying on green plants for life.

What are food chains and webs?

The only source of energy available to life on Earth is the Sun. Food chain and web diagrams are illustrations that show how energy that is trapped by plants is passed on to animals. All food chains and webs start with plants.

Which plants grow in the sea?

Animals that live in the sea rely on plants for life too. Some graze on seaweeds like these. Others feed on microscopic plants that float in the sea (called algae), or they eat animals that eat those algae.

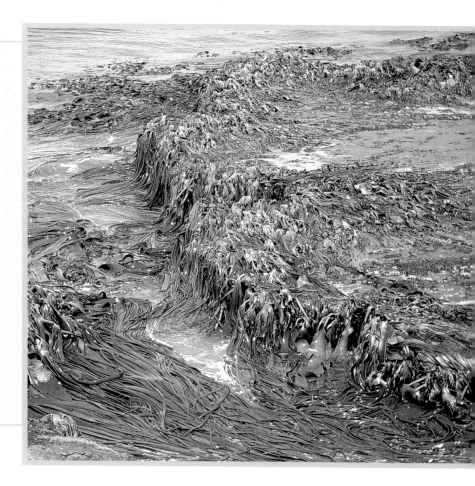

What are the parts of a plant?

There are more than 300,000 different kinds of plants in the world and they come in many different shapes, sizes and colours. Yet even though they look so different, most plants are made up of the same basic parts. Each part of a plant has an important job to do.

Most plants have **roots** that hold them in the ground. The stem holds the other parts of the plant up. Leaves are the parts of the plant that trap sunlight and use it to make food in the form of sugars. Most of the green plants in the world also have flowers. Flowers are the parts that a plant uses to **reproduce**. Flowers make **seeds** that can grow into new plants.

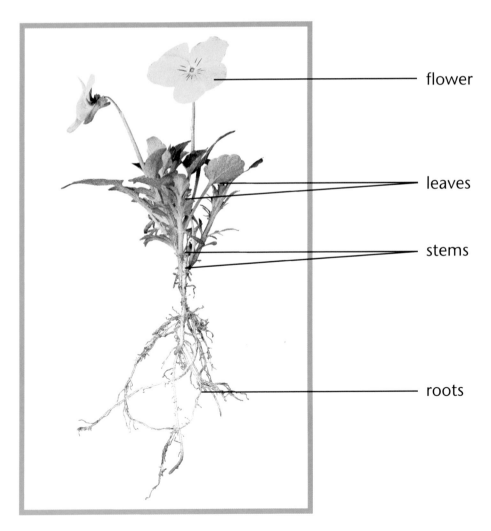

flower

leaves

stems

roots

How do leaves make food?

A plant makes its food inside its **leaves** by a process called **photosynthesis**. Leaves are often called the plant's food factory. Like all factories, leaves need a source of power – sunlight provides them with this power. Leaves grow high up on a **stem** and many are broad and flat so that they can catch as much light as possible. Leaves are often also darker on the upper side than the lower side. This is because there is more **chlorophyll** in the upper side, as it takes in more light.

How do leaves capture light?

Leaves are arranged on a plant so that they catch as much light as possible. If you look up into a tree, you will see that even though there are lots of leaves, they are very spread out and not many of them really overlap.

What does photosynthesis mean?

Photosynthesis is the name for the way plants make food. The word means 'making with light' ('photo' means light and 'synthesis' means 'to make'). Leaves use light to make food for the plant.

What do leaves use to make food?

The ingredients a leaf uses to make food are **carbon dioxide** and water. Carbon dioxide is a gas in the air. Leaves collect it through hundreds of tiny holes called **stomata**. Most plants get the water they need from the ground. They suck it in through their **roots** and it travels through tubes within the root and the stem up into the leaves.

How many stomata do leaves have?

There may be hundreds of stomata on the underside of a leaf, but you cannot normally see them because they are so tiny. They are magnified (made bigger) in this picture so that you can see them.

How does photosynthesis work?

Water is made up of two different **elements** – hydrogen and **oxygen**. In photosynthesis, a leaf uses **energy** trapped by the chlorophyll from sunlight to split water into these two separate parts. Then it mixes the hydrogen with the carbon dioxide to make food (in the form of sugars) for the leaf. Oxygen is released into the air through the stomata.

How do plants use the food?

The plant uses some of the sugars made in its leaves straight away to provide the energy it needs to grow. Plants also store some food to use later – for example, to make flowers in summertime. In most plants the food is carried from the leaves to other parts through tubes that go all round the plant's body, rather like the blood vessels in our bodies.

How do plants store food?

Plants often store food in underground plant parts, such as a root or an underground stem. Potatoes and carrots are underground food stores. When we eat these vegetables, we use the food stored in them for ourselves!

Leaf skeletons

When a leaf dies, the green parts rot away first and leave a leaf skeleton like this. This network of tubes supports a leaf. It carries water to the leaf and sugars away from it.

EXPERIMENT: Do plants grow towards light?

HYPOTHESIS:
Most plants need light for photosynthesis. Without it, they would die. Try this experiment to see how hard a plant will work to make sure it gets the light it needs.

EQUIPMENT:
A small pot plant with a strong tight root system, five or six large sponges, string and water. Try to use a smallish plant with soft stems, such as basil or broad bean.

EXPERIMENT STEPS:

1 Take the plant out of the pot, leaving as much soil around the roots as you can.
2 Wet the sponges and wrap them all around the roots and mud, including the flat part around the stem. Tie the sponges on with the string.
3 Carefully turn the plant upside-down and use the string to hang it by a sunny window.
4 Check the plant every day and keep the sponges damp.
5 Write down what you see.

CONCLUSION:
You should see that the leaves and stems of your plant grow in the direction of the sunlight, even if they have to twist and turn in rather odd ways!

How do plants take in water?

The larger **roots** of a plant hold the plant firmly in place even in high winds. Smaller roots grow out from these tough large roots. Tiny root hairs grow out of the sides of the smaller roots, and these have the job of sucking up water from the ground. Plants have lots of these root hairs to increase the amount of water they can take in. The hairs are small enough to grow around the little pieces in soil, to reach the droplets of water between them.

Why do plants wilt?

Plants need water because they are mostly made up of water, like most living things. Water supports plant parts such as **stems** and helps them stand up. When these parts do not get enough water, they wilt or droop.

Root hairs

After root hairs collect water, they pass it on to the main roots, which then supply the plant with the water it needs to live.

What else does a plant need to live?

Just as people need different kinds of food to be healthy, plants need different kinds of food too. Plants get most of the **nutrients** they need from the food that they make in their **leaves**, but they get other nutrients from the soil. When roots take in water, they also take in **minerals** and nutrients that have soaked into the water from the soil. These things help plants to grow and be healthy.

What is soil made of?

Soil is partly made up of very small pieces of rock. Minerals from these rock pieces wash into water that is in the soil. Soil also contains nutrients that have seeped into the ground from dead plants and animals that have rotted.

Storing water

In hot places without much rain, plants have different ways of surviving. This 'elephant's foot' tree in Madagascar stores its water in a fat, swollen stem.

How do roots take in water?

Plant roots suck up water by **transpiration**. This process works in much the same way as when you drink using a straw. When you suck water from the top of the straw, it causes more water to fill the space left at the bottom of the straw. In plants, tubes starting in the roots take water all the way up into the leaves.

Water passes out of the leaves through the **stomata**. This causes more water to flow in to the bottom of the tubes in the roots to replace it. Water escapes from the leaves because it **evaporates**. As sunshine warms the leaves, the water inside them warms up too. This makes some of the water turn into a gas called water vapour. This gas passes out of the stomata into the air.

Inside a root

This magnified picture shows the tubes inside a root. These tubes run through the root, up the stem and into the leaves.

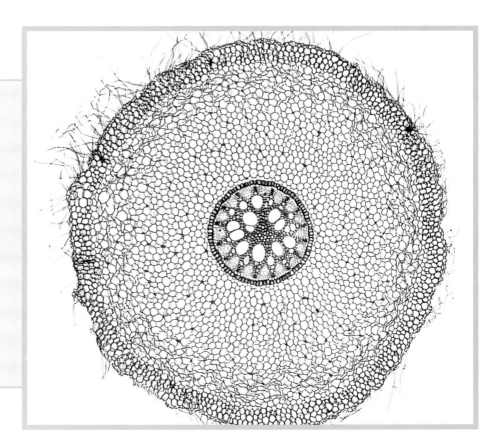

13

EXPERIMENT: Find out about transpiration.

HYPOTHESIS:
You can prove that plants use transpiration to suck up water through their roots by doing this simple experiment.

EQUIPMENT:
A clear plastic bag, string or a plastic tie and a pot plant with lots of leaves.

EXPERIMENT STEPS:
1 One morning, put the plastic bag over part of the plant. Leave it in a sunny spot such as a windowsill.
2 Tie the bag on tightly at the end, making sure it does not squash the leaves.
3 Look at the inside of the bag the next morning.
4 Write down what you see.

CONCLUSION:
You should see drops of water on the inside of the bag. If it was hot the day before, there may be quite a bit of water. The water inside the leaves has evaporated through the stomata, and into the air in the bag. The water vapour (gas) then cooled overnight and turned back into droplets of water!

How do plants make seeds?

Most plants make **seeds** in their flowers. Flowers usually have male and female parts. In order to produce a seed, a **sex cell** from the male part of a flower has to fuse (join together) with a sex cell from the female part of another flower. This fused cell then grows into a seed.

What are the parts of a flower?

The parts of a flower that help it to **reproduce** are usually found in the centre of its petals. The female part is called the **carpel**. At the base of the carpel is an **ovary**. This holds the female sex cells and is where the seed grows. The **stigma** is the sticky top part of the carpel. The male part of the flower is called the **stamen**. The male sex cells are in the **anthers**, at the top of each stamen. Each male sex cell is stored inside a **pollen** grain. This tulip flower has been cut open to show its different reproductive parts.

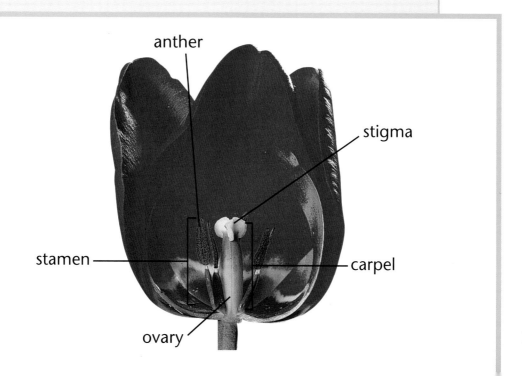

What is pollination?

The first step in seed production is getting the pollen from the stamens on to a carpel. This is called **pollination**. Plants are rooted to the ground and cannot move. They need help to pass on their pollen, for example, from insects, other animals, or the wind.

How does animal pollination work?

Flowers have colourful petals and sweet scents to attract insects, bats and some birds to come to feed on their nectar. Nectar is a sweet liquid that flowers store at the base of their petals. For example, when bees crawl into a flower to feed on the nectar, they brush against the anthers and pollen sticks to their bodies. When they stop off at another flower to feed, some of the pollen rubs off on to the sticky stigma at the top of the carpel of that new flower.

Sipping nectar

In some places, bats, birds and other animals will also help to pollinate plants. When a hummingbird reaches its long beak into a hibiscus flower to sip **nectar**, pollen brushes on to its chin. When it rubs off on a different flower it results in **fertilization**.

What is wind pollination?

Flowering plants such as grass, which use wind for pollination, do not have bright petals and scents, as they do not need to attract insects. The important thing about wind-pollinated flowers is that they grow where the wind can easily catch them. Most have anthers that grow at the end of long stalks and their pollen is very light. The stigmas on wind-pollinated plants are usually quite big and feathery, so that they can sweep up pollen if it blows past them.

Clouds of pollen

Grasses that use the wind for pollination produce so much pollen that it can look like clouds of dust blowing from the plants on a windy summer's day.

What happens next?

After a pollen grain has landed on the stigma of another flower, it grows a tiny tube into the stigma and down into the ovary. Then, the male sex cell slides out of the pollen grain, down the tube and into the ovary. Here it joins with the female sex cell. When they join, we say the female sex cell has been fertilized. Now it can grow into a seed.

What are fruits?

After fertilization, most parts of the flower die and drop off the plant. Only the ovary remains. It swells to form a protective case around the growing seed. This is called a **fruit**.

Do all green plants make seeds in flowers?

Conifers are trees with needle-like **leaves** that make seeds in **cones** instead of flowers. Conifers have both male cones and female cones. Seeds grow inside a female cone that has been fertilized and the cone protects the seeds until they are ready to leave the parent plant. Some other types of plants do not make seeds, but reproduce in different ways.

How do seeds grow?

To grow well, **seeds** need to get away from their parent plant to find a new patch of ground where there is space and light. This is why seeds grow in **fruits**. Fruits protect seeds as they develop and then help them to move away from the parent plant. Some fruits are fleshy and soft; some are dry and hard.

What are fleshy fruits?

Plums, cherries, apricots, melons and tomatoes are all kinds of fleshy fruits. The soft, juicy fruits get bigger as the seed or seeds inside them grow. When the seeds are ready to leave the parent plant, the fruits become ripe. Their bright colours and enticing smells tempt animals, including humans, to eat them. Later on, the seeds fall to the ground in the animal's droppings, or are spat out somewhere new.

Helping seeds to grow

When seeds fall to the ground in an animal's droppings, the droppings supply them with nutrients, helping them grow!

What are dry fruits?

Dry fruits do not have sweet soft flesh, but they come in many different shapes and forms. Some dry fruits, like peas, have pods. These fruits spread seeds when they dry out and twist until the pod suddenly splits open, scattering the seeds around. Some plants (such as sycamore trees) have fruits shaped like wings, which help them to float away on the wind. Some plants (such as alder trees) that live near rivers have fruits that can float, so that the water spreads their seeds.

Seeds that can fly!

Sycamore (seen here) and maple fruits have two wing-shaped parts that make them spin and fly as they fall from the tree, often carrying the seeds far from the parent plant.

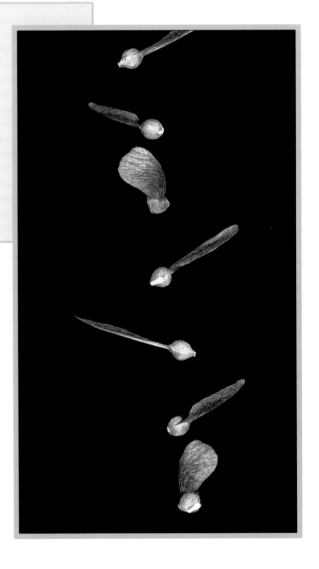

Animals help to spread the seeds of dry fruits too. In autumn, when squirrels bury acorns and other nuts to eat in winter, they forget where they have put all of them. In spring, those left in the ground find themselves in the perfect place to grow!

How do seeds grow?

Different seeds need different conditions to grow, but many wait until spring when it is warmer and there are more hours of daylight. Inside a seed there is a tiny baby plant that consists of a tiny **root** and a **shoot**, and a store of food. The seed has a tough outer coat that stops it drying out while it waits and the baby plant lives on the food store.

When the time is right, the seed soaks up water from the soil around it. Then the young root and shoot swell up and grow out of the seed. Above the ground, the shoot becomes a **stem** and grows **leaves**. Now the new plant can use the leaves to make its own food, so that it can grow bigger and bigger. The root grows longer below the ground.

Starting to grow

This horse chestnut seed is just starting to grow. Roots grow out of a seed and down into the soil. Shoots grow up towards the light.

EXPERIMENT: What do seeds need to grow?

HYPOTHESIS:
Seeds need light and water to grow.

EQUIPMENT:
Packet of cress seeds, four sheets of kitchen paper, four clean empty margarine tubs and an old shoebox.

EXPERIMENT STEPS:

1 Fold each sheet of paper twice or three times so it fits into a tub. Place one in each tub.
2 Add a little water to two tubs to dampen the paper. Leave two tubs dry.
3 Sprinkle a pinch of cress seeds into each tub.
4 Put one wet and one dry tub on a windowsill. Put one wet and one dry tub inside the shoebox.
5 Check the tubs after a few days and write down what you see.

CONCLUSION:
The seeds in the dry tubs will not start growing, because they need water to do so. The seeds on wet paper in the shoebox should start to grow, but the plants will be pale and unhealthy. Seeds can start to grow in the dark (after all, it is dark underground) but leaves need light to make food for the plant to grow. The seeds on wet paper in the light on the windowsill should be the healthiest.

Why are plants different?

One of the reasons that plants look so different is that they grow all over the world and in many different kinds of **habitat**. Plants grow in ways and forms that help them survive in the particular conditions their habitat provides.

How do plants cope with heat?

Tropical rainforests grow in the warmest, wettest parts of the world. Rainforest trees grow faster and taller than just about anywhere else – mahogany and teak grow up to 50 metres tall. These giants have huge flared **roots** that extend above the ground to help hold them up. Deserts are even hotter, but they are also dry. Many desert plants have fleshy **stems** that can expand to store water when it rains.

Why are cacti spiky?

Desert plants like this cactus have **leaves** shaped like spikes, to reduce the amount of water lost through **transpiration** and to stop animals stealing the water stored in their fleshy stems!

How do plants in cold places look?

Plants grow even in the coldest parts of the world, such as mountain tops and around the North Pole. In icy places, water turns to ice quickly, so life is hard for plants.

Most plants that grow in cold places grow low to the ground, out of the path of icy winds. For example, willow trees are usually tall, but Arctic willows never grow bigger than 10 centimetres! Some plants in cold places grow in compact forms, like cushions or mats, very close to the ground. The outer leaves form a dome over the plant that traps warmth and moisture beneath. Some small flowering plants have fine, hair-like strands on their leaves and stems to trap warmth, rather like fur.

What is special about conifer leaves?

Conifer trees, like these Ponderosa pines, can live in cold places. Their needle-like leaves reduce the amount of water they lose, and a thin layer of **wax** around them protects them from cold and snow.

How do plants in water grow?

Plants that grow in ponds and rivers look different because they have to find ways of staying near the surface to get light. Plants that have their roots in the soil at the bottom of the pond or river have long, floating leaves on tall stems to hold their leaves up to the light. Some water plants float on the surface. They have tiny roots that dangle below the surface and take the **nutrients** they need from the water.

Why does seaweed look different?

Seaweed has parts called holdfasts that look rather like roots, but they only hold the plant to rocks. They do not take in nutrients. Seaweed absorbs the water and nutrients it needs from the seawater around it through leaf-like parts called fronds.

Floating leaves

Water lilies have wide, floating leaves that can stay on top of the water to catch light even if their roots are in the bottom of the pond.

25

When do plants change?

Plants go on growing throughout their lives, so they change constantly as they get slightly bigger every year. Plants also change with the seasons. Some plants only change a little in different seasons, whilst others change a lot.

Deciduous plants change in autumn to avoid the cold harsh weather of winter. They lose their **leaves** and sometimes all their parts that are above ground. They rest through winter, living on food stored in underground parts such as **roots** and **bulbs**. Then they use this food to help them grow again in spring.

Why do leaves change colour in autumn?

The leaves of deciduous trees contain many colours, but in spring and summer the green **chlorophyll** hides them. In autumn, the chlorophyll breaks down because the tree stops making food and growing, so the trees' other colours – reds, oranges and yellows – show through.

Autumn colour

Leaves that fall from deciduous trees in autumn form a colourful carpet on the woodland floor, as in this woodland of common beech trees in Northumberland, England.

Most **conifers** are evergreens – plants that do not lose all their leaves in autumn. Their needles, which are covered in a coating of **wax**, are tough enough to survive the winter cold. However, even these plants change in spring and summer. This is when conifers make lots of new leaves and also **cones** that can produce **seeds**.

Why do woodland flowers grow in spring?

Flowering plants, such as bluebells, which grow in deciduous woodland, survive winter as underground bulbs. They burst into flower the following spring, before the trees above fill with leaves and take all the sunlight.

What happens when plants die?

When plants die, they begin to decay (rot). **Bacteria**, **fungi** and tiny animals such as insects eat parts of them and the rest gradually breaks down into smaller and smaller pieces. These wash into the soil with rainwater. These changes are a vital part of nature. The **nutrients** that were in the plants become part of the soil, so that new plants can use them to grow.

People who found the answers

Sir Joseph Banks (1744-1820)

Sir Joseph Banks (shown here) is one of the most famous botanists (plant scientists) in history. He explored the world looking for new plants. In 1786, he sailed with Captain Cook to Tahiti and the South Seas, and took part in the first exploration of Australia. There, he discovered many plants that were new to the Western world, including the beautiful banksia plants, which were named after him. He was President of the Royal Society, the most important British scientific society, and he had a huge natural history collection.

Sir Joseph Dalton Hooker (1817-1911)

Sir Joseph Dalton Hooker was the one of the most important botanists of the 19th century. He was interested in plants from a very young age and attended botany lectures given by his father (also a famous botanist) from the age of seven! Hooker travelled around the world, collecting and drawing new plants. He was a close friend and adviser of Charles Darwin, and he eventually became the director of Britain's Royal Botanical Gardens at Kew in London.

Amazing facts

- Plants give us life! During **photosynthesis**, plants release **oxygen** gas through their **stomata**. Oxygen is a vital part of the air that we need to breathe. Plants are also the basis of every food chain in the world, and without them people would not have any food to eat.

- Plants reduce air pollution! By taking in **carbon dioxide** to make their food by photosynthesis, plants help to remove this gas from the air. If there were too much carbon dioxide in the air, it would be poisonous to us.

- Plants are the biggest living things on Earth. Giant redwood trees, like these in Sequoia National Park, California, USA, weigh in at 2500 tonnes, over ten times heavier than the largest animal in the world, the blue whale.

- On a hot day, a large tree takes in enough water to fill about five bathtubs! It has to take in this much to replace the water that **evaporates** through its **leaves**.

- Flowers that use wind for **pollination** make an incredible number of **pollen** grains. Just one birch catkin may make five and a half million pollen grains! Wind-pollinated flowers make so much pollen because most of it is wasted.

Glossary

anthers swollen tips of a stamen that contain pollen grains

bacteria microscopic living things, some of which decompose (break down) dead organisms and waste

bulb underground bud protected by fleshy leaves. An onion is a kind of bulb.

carbon dioxide gas found in small amounts in air. Plants use it for photosynthesis.

carpel female part of a flower

chlorophyll green substance in plants that is used for photosynthesis

cones form of dry fruit in which conifer seeds develop. Cones are often egg-shaped, with overlapping woody scales.

conifer tree that has cones and needle-like leaves that it replaces gradually all year round

consumers living things that cannot make their own food but must consume other organisms in order to live

deciduous describes plants that lose all their leaves by winter and grow new ones in spring

elements everything is made up of substances called elements. Some things are made up of one kind of element, such as oxygen. Others, such as water, are made up of several elements.

energy all living things need energy to live, grow and repair themselves if injured

evaporate to turn from a liquid to a gas. Clothes on a line dry because water evaporates from them.

fertilization/fertilize when a male sex cell fuses (joins) with a female sex cell and begins to form a seed

fruit scientific name for the part of a flowering plant in which its seeds develop

fungi group of living things, some of which look like plants, but which cannot make their own food by photosynthesis. Mushrooms and toadstools are kinds of fungi.

habitat natural home of a group of plants and animals

kingdoms name for the five groups that living things are divided into: plants, animals, fungi, protists and bacteria

leaves plant parts that catch sunlight and carry out photosynthesis

minerals chemical building block of rocks. Plants need some minerals to be healthy.

nectar sugary substance that plants make in their flowers to attract birds and insects, which eat it

nutrients chemicals that plants and animals get from their food that they need in order to live

ovary part of a flower that contains female sex cells

oxygen gas found in air. Many living things need oxygen to stay alive.

photosynthesis process by which leaves make food for their plants, using water, carbon dioxide and energy from sunlight

pollen tiny dust-like particles that contain a plant's male sex cells

pollination when pollen travels from the anthers of one flower to the stigma of the same or a different flower

producers living things that produce their own food within themselves

reproduce when a living thing produces young like itself

root part of a plant that usually grows underground to anchor it in the soil and take in water and nutrients

seed part made by flowers to grow into a new plant

sex cells special male or female cells that combine to make a young organism

shoot new stem growing from the main stem of a plant, or out of a seed

stamen male part of a flower

stem part of a plant that holds up leaves and flowers

stigma part of the flower that receives pollen in the process of pollination

stomata tiny openings on a leaf that are used to take in carbon dioxide

transpiration process by which roots take in water

wax natural, plastic-like substance. Plants often have a thin layer of wax around their leaves and/or fruits to stop them drying out.

Index

More books to read

The Life of Plants series, Louise and Richard Spilsbury
    (Heinemann Library, 2002)
The Oxford Children's Encyclopedia of Plants and Animals
    (Oxford University Press, 2000)

Titles in the *Science Answers* series include:

Hardback   0 431 17512 8

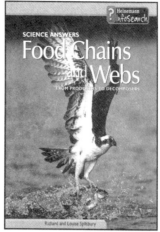

Hardback   0 431 17513 6

Hardback   0 431 17514 4

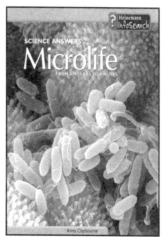

Hardback   0 431 17515 2

Hardback   0 431 17516 0

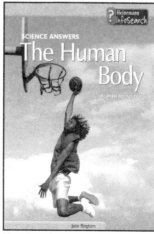

Hardback   0 431 17517 9

Find out about the other titles in this series on our website www.heinemann.co.uk/library